I didn't know that

dinosaurs
laid
eggs

© Aladdin Books Ltd 1997
© U.S. text 1997
Produced by
Aladdin Books Ltd
28 Percy Street
London W1P 0LD

First published in the United States in 1997 by
Copper Beech Books,
an imprint of
The Millbrook Press
2 Old New Milford Road
Brookfield, Connecticut 06804

Concept, editorial, and design by
David West Children's Books

Designer: Robert Perry
Illustrators: James Field—Simon Girling and Associates, Mike Lacy
Jo Moore

Printed in Belgium
Library of Congress Cataloging-in-Publication Data
Petty, Kate.
Dinosaurs laid eggs : and other amazing facts about prehistoric reptiles /
Kate Petty ; illustrated by James Field, Mike Lacy, and Jo Moore.
p. cm. — (I didn't know that —)
Includes index.
Summary: Presents facts about the appearance, size, and behavior of dinosaurs
and other prehistoric reptiles.
ISBN 0-7613-0549-1 (lib. bdg.). — ISBN 0-7613-0596-3 (trade HC)
1. Dinosaurs—Miscellanea—Juvenile literature. [1. Dinosaurs.]
I. Field, James, 1959- ill. II. Lacey, Mike, ill. III. Moore, Jo, ill.
IV. Title. V. Series.
QE862.D5P483 1997   97-8021
567.9—dc21   CIP AC

I didn't know that dinosaurs laid eggs

Kate Petty

COPPER BEECH BOOKS
BROOKFIELD, CONNECTICUT

I didn't know that

True or false?
Humans were responsible for
making the dinosaurs extinct.

Answer: **False**
Humans and dinosaurs never lived
together on Earth. Over 60 million
years separate the last dinosaurs and
our earliest ancestors.

One Million Years B.C. – the
film that got it wrong!

Saltasaurus

Dinosaur history is divided into three
periods: Triassic (early), Jurassic
(middle), and Cretaceous (late). Different
dinosaurs lived in different periods.

Coelophysis

Tyrannosaurus   Stegosaurus

Cretaceous	Jurassic	Triassic

Crocodiles have hardly changed at all since dinosaur times.

One of the differences between dinosaurs and other reptile families, such as crocodiles or lizards, is that dinosaurs walked on straight legs.

A dinosaur's skin would have been very tough and scaly to the touch. Like a snake's skin, which people sometimes expect to be slimy, it would in fact have felt dry and bumpy.

Close-up of
T. rex's skin

I didn't know that

dinosaur means "terrible lizard."

By 1841 people realized that these enormous fossilized bones belonged to huge extinct reptiles, not giant humans! A scientist named Dr. Richard Owen named them "dino" (terrible) "saurs" (lizards).

Tyrannosaurus rex

Thirty-nine feet tall with a three-foot-wide mouth and teeth as long as carving knives, *Tyrannosaurus rex* was a nightmare lizard! Its name means King Tyrant Lizard.

T. rex's fossilized tooth

The first dinosaur discovered in the West was found in 1824.

I didn't know that some dinosaurs were bigger than a four-story building. *Ultrasauros* was a huge *sauropod*, the biggest dinosaur ever, at 98 feet long and 39 feet high. A human would barely have reached its ankles!

Compsognathus

SEARCH & FIND FIND & SEARCH

Can you find nine *Compsognathuses?*

Ultrasauros

Fossilized footprints show that the enormous sauropods moved in groups, walking with long strides. Some might have swum across rivers, pulling themselves along with their front legs.

The chicken-sized *Compsognathus* was one of the smallest dinosaurs. It was a speedy meat-eater, which chased after tiny mammals, lizards, and insects.

Mamenchisaurus had a 33-foot-long neck!

Deinocheirus

A hug from *Deinocheirus*, "terrible hand," would have been deadly! Its arms were over eight feet long. This birdlike creature was probably bigger than *T. rex*

Tenontosaurus

All meat-eating dinosaurs were *theropods*, with three toes and long claws. Most walked on two legs.

SEARCH & FIND & FIND & SEARCH & FIND & SEARCH &

Can you find the *Tenontosaurus* that got away?

Deinonychus

I didn't know that

some dinosaurs hunted in packs. Fossils have been found of a group of *Deinonychuses* surrounding a *Tenontosaurus*, a *herbivore*. They probably hunted it together like lions or wolves do today.

Deinonychus had long claws for stabbing and cutting. On each hind foot it had a special slashing claw, which could be pulled back when it ran.

Sauropods (like *Diplodocus* and *Apatosaurus*) had teeth like pegs for raking leaves or spoon-shaped ones for pulling leaves off a plant. They swallowed without chewing.

Apatosaurus

I didn't know that

most dinosaurs ate plants. The earliest dinosaurs were meat-eaters, but by the Jurassic period plant-eaters were flourishing. There was still no grass to graze on – instead they grazed on other plants.

Big plant-eating dinosaurs had to eat 400 pounds of leaves a day!

Scientists can also learn about dinosaur diets from their fossilized droppings, which might contain seeds, leaves, or fish scales.

Hadrosaurs (duckbills like *Parasaurolophus* and *Edmontosaurus*) could eat Christmas trees! They ground twigs and pine needles between jaws that contained more than a thousand teeth, pressed together into ridged plates.

Edmontosaurus

Centrosaurus

Ceratopsian dinosaurs (like *Centrosaurus*) had parrotlike beaks for cropping very tough plants, with strong jaws and sharp teeth for cutting them up.

15

I didn't know that

some dinosaurs went fishing. *Baryonyx*, "heavy claw," was discovered in 1983. It had unusually long, curved claws and a fossilized fish in its stomach. Scientists thought that the claws were used for hooking fish out of the water.

Baryonyx

Millions of years after the crime, a fossilized *Oviraptor*, "egg thief," was caught! It had a telltale pair of prongs in its otherwise toothless mouth. They were probably used for cracking the eggs it stole.

True or false?
Some dinosaurs had no teeth at all.

Answer: **True**
The birdlike *Gallimimus,* an *ornithopod,* had no teeth. Twice the size of an ostrich, it fed on insects and anything it could swallow whole.

Like snakes, dinosaurs also swallowed a meal without chewing. The fossilized skeleton of a *Compsognathus* (see page 11) was discovered with a fossilized whole lizard in its stomach.

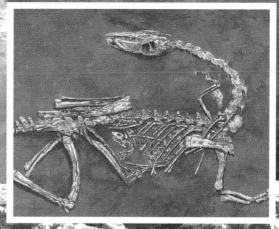

I didn't know that

dinosaurs laid eggs. They did—just like all reptiles. The dinosaur mother would scrape out a hollow nest in the ground and cover the eggs to keep them warm. She would bring food to her babies until they could leave the nest.

True or false?
The biggest dinosaurs laid giant eggs three feet long.

Answer: **False**

Even the biggest dinosaur eggs were no more than five times the size of a chicken's egg. A bigger egg would need to have a thicker shell. This would suffocate the baby.

SEARCH & FIND
FIND & SEARCH
Can you find the imposter?

Maiasaura

Fossilized footprints of small tracks surrounded by larger ones show that young dinosaurs on the move were protected by the older, larger ones.

! Like a cuckoo, the *Troodon* may have laid its eggs in others' nests.

Carnotaurus

I didn't know that

some dinosaurs were armor-plated. This was protection from the fierce meat-eaters such as *Carnotaurus* that hunted them. Like armadillos and porcupines today, certain plant-eaters had tough skins or spikes.

Euoplocephalus

Euoplocephalus even had bony eyelids! It also had spikes and a lethal clubbed tail for defense – enough to make any predator think twice.

20

Tyrannosaurus rex

Sauropods were protected by sheer size, but a group of *Triceratops* could make a wall of horns that would scare off their enemies.

Triceratops

True or false?
The spiny plates on a *Stegosaurus* (right) were for protection.

Answer: **False**

They were probably for controlling its body heat. Blood so near the skin's surface could warm up very quickly in the Sun or cool down in the shade.

Diplodocus used its tail as a defensive whip.

I didn't know that

some dinosaurs had head-butting contests. Like rams and stags today, "*boneheads*" such as *Stegoceras* battled for leadership. Their skulls were 10 inches thick, so it probably didn't hurt too much.

Parasaurolophus

Stegoceras

Some duck-billed dinosaurs, like *Parasaurolophus,* had hollow headpieces that were connected to their nasal passages. They might have snored! They didn't use their crests for fighting head to head.

SEARCH & FIND & FIND SEARCH & Can you find the chameleon?

No one knows what colors dinosaurs were. Like reptiles and birds today, they were probably colored to blend in with their surroundings. Like chameleons, some might have changed color.

True or false?

Pterosaurs had feathers.

Answer: **False**

More like bats than birds, pterosaurs like *Dimorphodon* had furry bodies and leathery wings. They had beaked faces, but they also had teeth.

Dimorphodon

Rhamphorynchus

Pteranodon

I didn't know that

Quetzalcoatlus was bigger than a hang glider. With a wingspan of 32 feet, it was the biggest creature ever to take to the air, gliding on warm air currents. Flying reptiles were not dinosaurs but *pterosaurs*.

The winged dinosaur, *Archaeopteryx*, was probably the first bird.

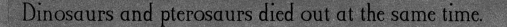

Quetzalcoatlus

Pteranodon swooped down from the cliff tops to catch fish from the sea. The crest on its head helped it to steer.

Pterodaustro also ate fish. It had a sieve in its beak so it could strain tiny fish as it flew low over the water.

I didn't know that

there were real sea monsters in dinosaur times. Dinosaurs didn't live in the sea, but it was full of all sorts of other huge and strange-looking swimming reptiles. They fed on fish and shellfish.

Elasmosaurus

The *plesiosaur Elasmosaurus* was 50 feet long and nearly all neck. Swimming through the water, it must have looked like *Diplodocus* with flippers!

The turtlelike *Archelon* was longer than a rowboat.

Ichthyosaurs were some of the earliest sea reptiles. They looked like dolphins and, like them, breathed air. They fed on the *ammonites* and *belemnites* you often find as fossils today.

Ichthyosaurs

Liopleurodon was one of the short-necked plesiosaurs. It really was a monster – its head was seven feet long!

Mosasaurus

Mosasaurs were some of the last sea reptiles and, at 33 feet long, the largest lizards ever. They looked like dragons, but with flippers rather than legs.

Liopleurodon

Paleontologists piece together dinosaur bones into skeletons. Then they flesh out the skeletons. They have to guess the colors. Take your own dinosaur models and paint them. What colors will you choose and why?

I didn't know that

some dinosaurs had feathers.

A fossil of a feathered dinosaur was found in China in 1996. New discoveries can change the way we think about dinosaurs. Just imagine how different they would look with feathers!

Close-up view of feathers.

You will never be able to see moving, living dinosaurs in a zoo. But there are many exhibitions of lifelike, moving dinosaurs all over the world. Try to find the one nearest to you. Write to them for information and visit it if you can.

Even though the feathers were probably for warmth rather than for flying, this find makes it even more likely that modern birds are related to dinosaurs.

If you can't visit any moving dinosaurs you can see them at the movies.

Glossary

Ammonites
Prehistoric shellfish, commonly found as fossils.

Belemnites
Prehistoric bullet-shaped shellfish, also common fossils.

Boneheads
The nickname given to Pachycephalosaurs. They were two-legged dinosaurs with incredibly thick skulls.

Ceratopsians
Dinosaurs that had horns and a protective bony frill.

Fossils
The remains of living things that have been preserved in rock.

Hadrosaurs
Duck-billed dinosaurs, often with a crest on their head.

Herbivore
Any plant-eater at the time of the dinosaurs and today.

Ichthyosaurs
Dolphin-like sea reptiles that lived at the same time as dinosaurs.

Mosasaurs
Dragon-like sea reptiles that lived at the same time as dinosaurs.

Ornithopods

A group of dinosaurs that walked on two legs. Most were plant-eaters.

Paleontologists

Scientists who study the fossilized remains of extinct animals and plants.

Plesiosaurs

Sea reptiles with flippers rather than legs, that lived at the same time as dinosaurs.

Pterosaurs

A group of flying reptiles that lived at the same time as dinosaurs.

Sauropods

A group of long-necked, long-tailed, four-legged, plant-eating dinosaurs.

They included *Diplodocus* and *Apatosaurus*.

Theropods

A group of meat-eating dinosaurs. Most of them walked on two legs. They included *Deinonychus*.

Index

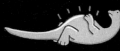